I Am an Artist

Janet Carson

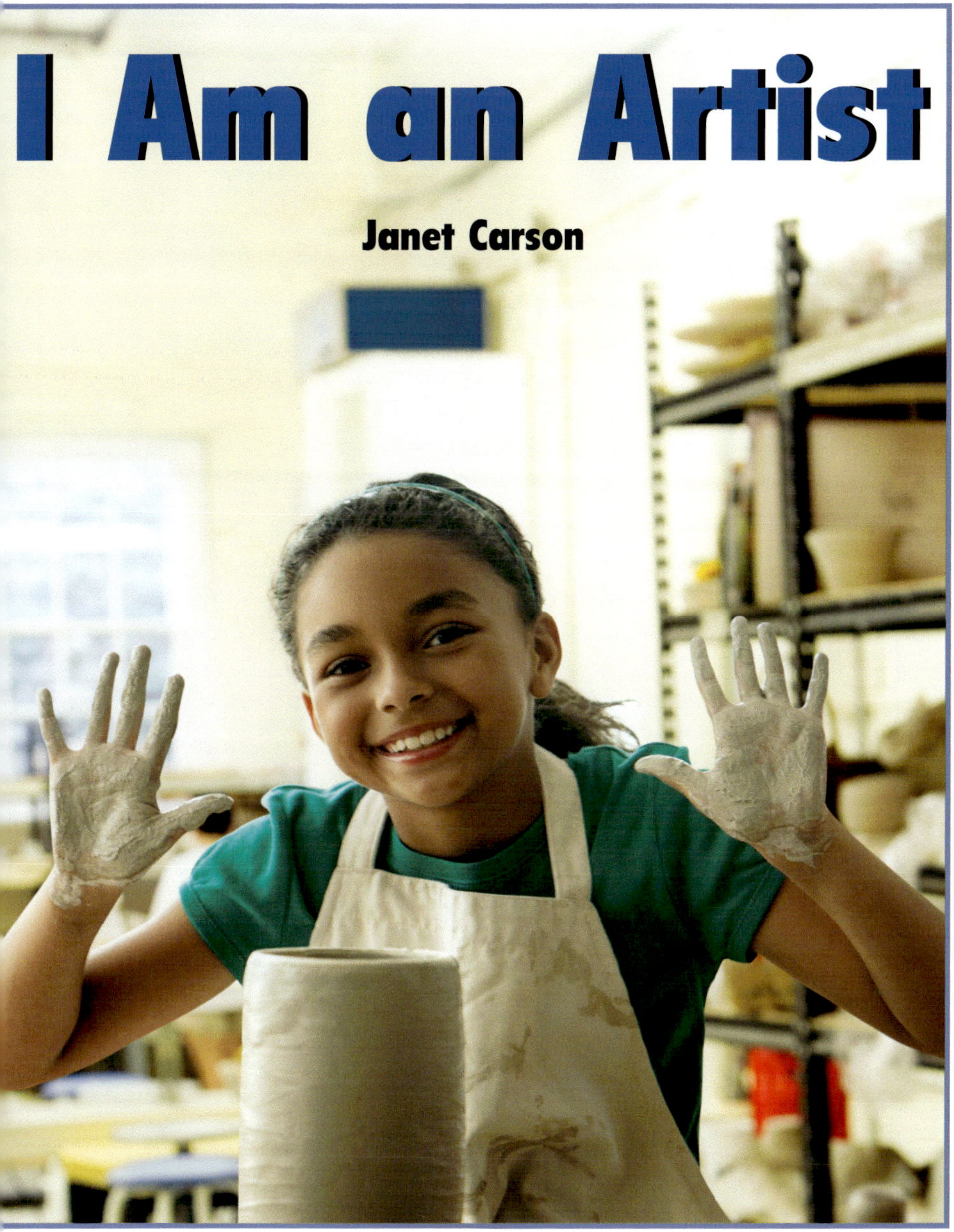

Rosen REAL READERS

Rosen Classroom Books & Materials
New York

I draw with a pencil.

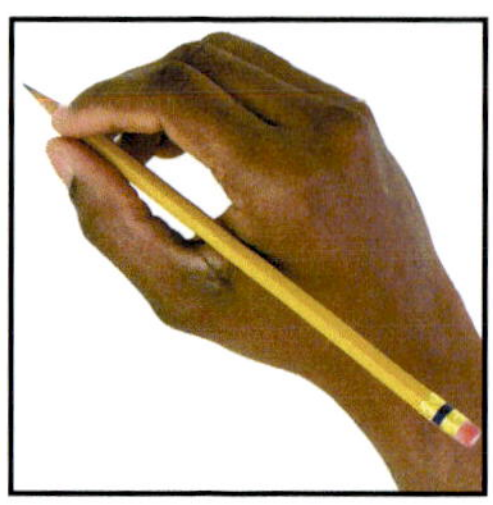

I draw with crayons.

I paint with a brush.

I paint with my fingers.

I make things with clay.

I make things with clay, too.

Words to Know

brush

clay

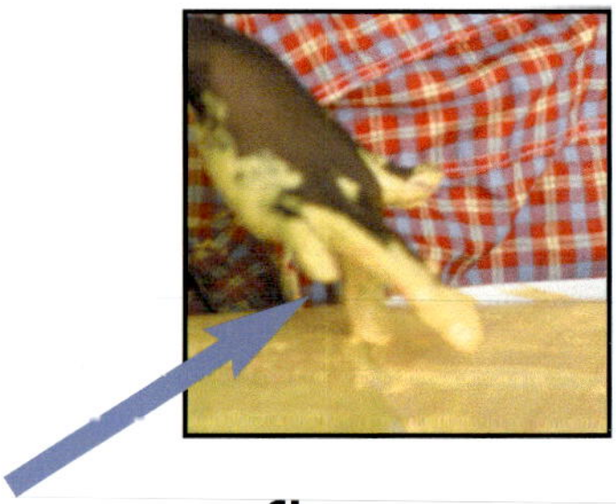

fingers

paint

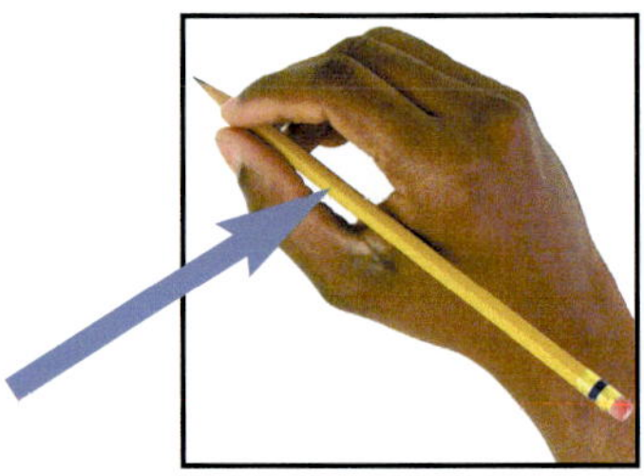

pencil